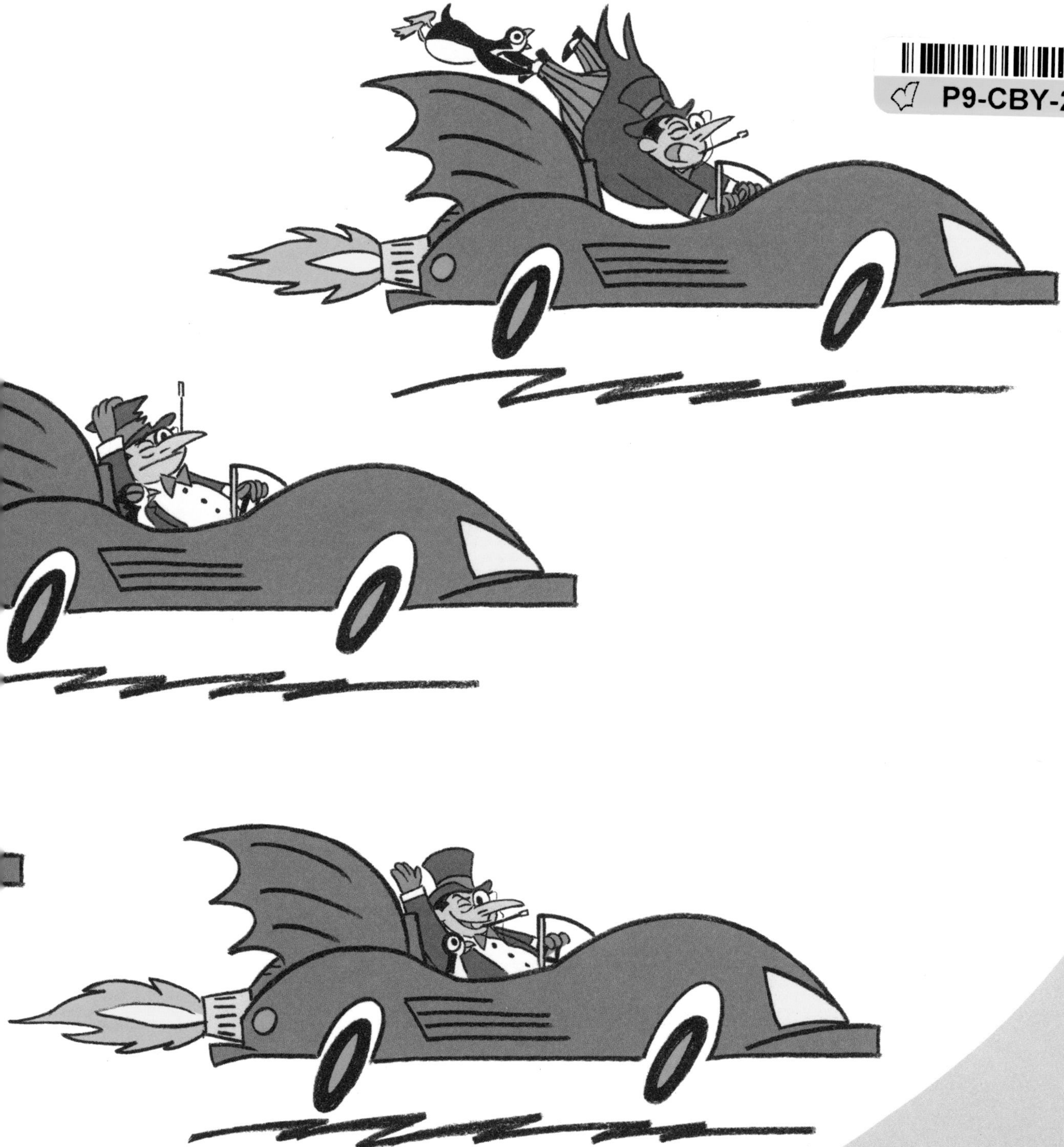

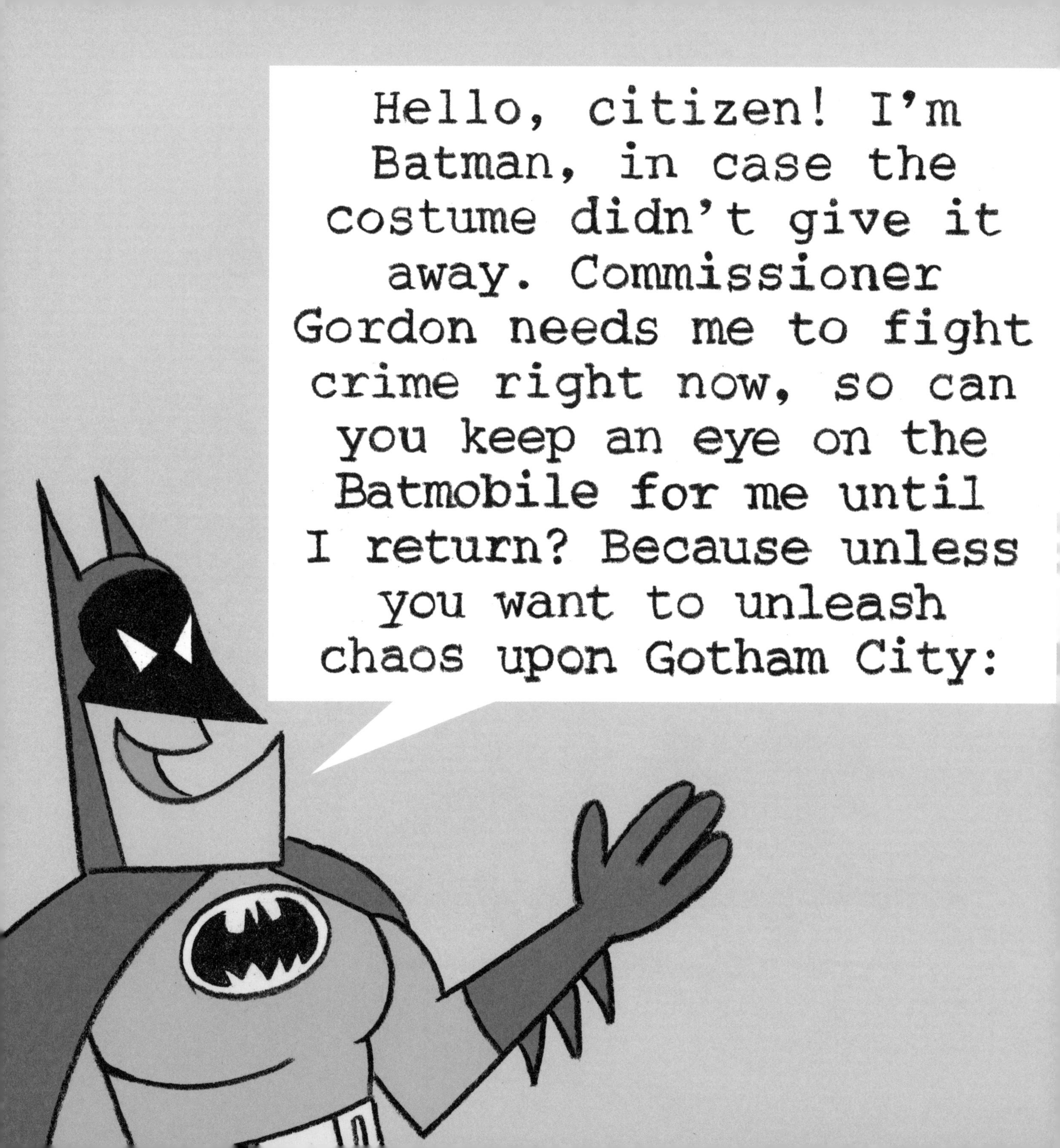
Hello, citizen! I'm Batman, in case the costume didn't give it away. Commissioner Gordon needs me to fight crime right now, so can you keep an eye on the Batmobile for me until I return? Because unless you want to unleash chaos upon Gotham City:

Don't Let the Penguin Drive the Batmobile!

words by jacob lambert · pictures by Tom Richmond

MAD BOOKS **William M. Gaines** Founder **John Ficarra** Senior VP & Executive Editor **Charlie Kadau, Joe Raiola, Dave Croatto** Senior Editors **Jacob Lambert** Associate Editor **Sam Viviano** VP – Art & Design **Ryan Flanders** Design Director **Patricia Dwyer** Assistant Art Director **Bernard Mendoza** Production Artist

Additional contributions by **Casey Boyd, Paula Sevenbergen,** and **Doug Thomson**

ADMINISTRATION **Dan DiDio** Publisher **Jim Lee** Publisher & Chief Creative Officer **Amit Desai** Executive VP – Business & Marketing Strategy, Direct to Consumer & Global Franchise Management **Bobbie Chase** VP & Executive Editor, Young Reader & Talent Development **Mark Chiarello** Senior VP – Art, Design & Collected Editions **John Cunningham** Senior VP – Sales & Trade Marketing **Briar Darden** VP – Business Affairs **Anne DePies** Senior VP – Business Strategy, Finance & Administration **Don Falletti** VP – Manufacturing Operations **Lawrence Ganem** VP – Editorial Administration & Talent Relations **Alison Gill** Senior VP – Manufacturing & Operations **Hank Kanalz** Senior VP – Editorial Strategy & Administration **Jay Kogan** Senior VP – Legal Affairs **Nick J. Napolitano** VP – Manufacturing Administration **Lisette Osterloh** VP – Digital Marketing & Events **Eddie Scannell** VP – Consumer Marketing **Courtney Simmons** Senior VP – Publicity & Communications **Jim (Ski) Sokolowski** VP – Comic Book Specialty Sales & Trade Marketing **Nancy Spears** VP – Mass, Book, Digital Sales & Trade Marketing **Michele R. Wells** VP – Content Strategy

Visit MAD online at: madmagazine.com

MIX
Paper from
responsible sources
FSC® C011825

for conor
and charlotte

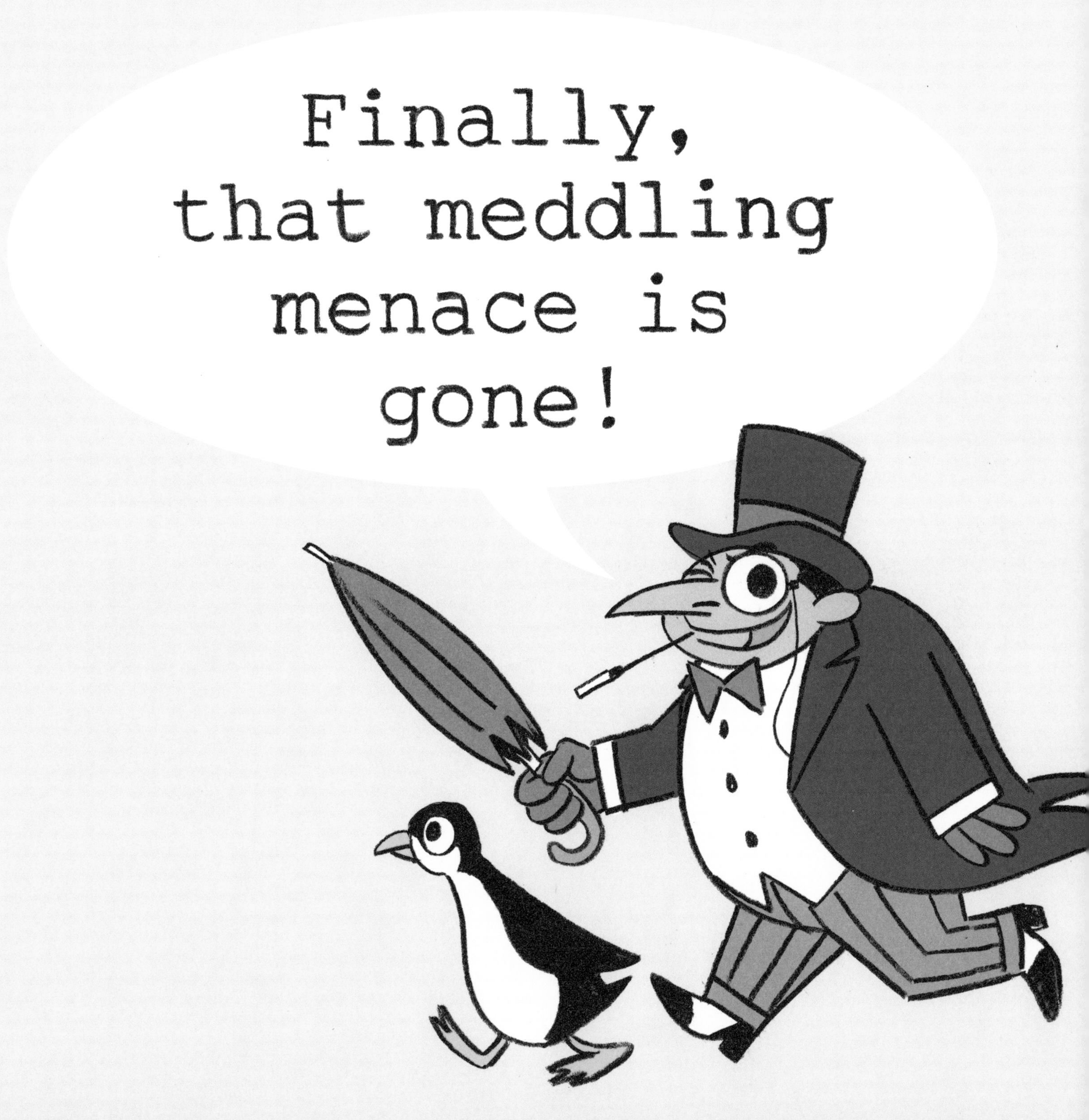
Finally, that meddling menace is gone!

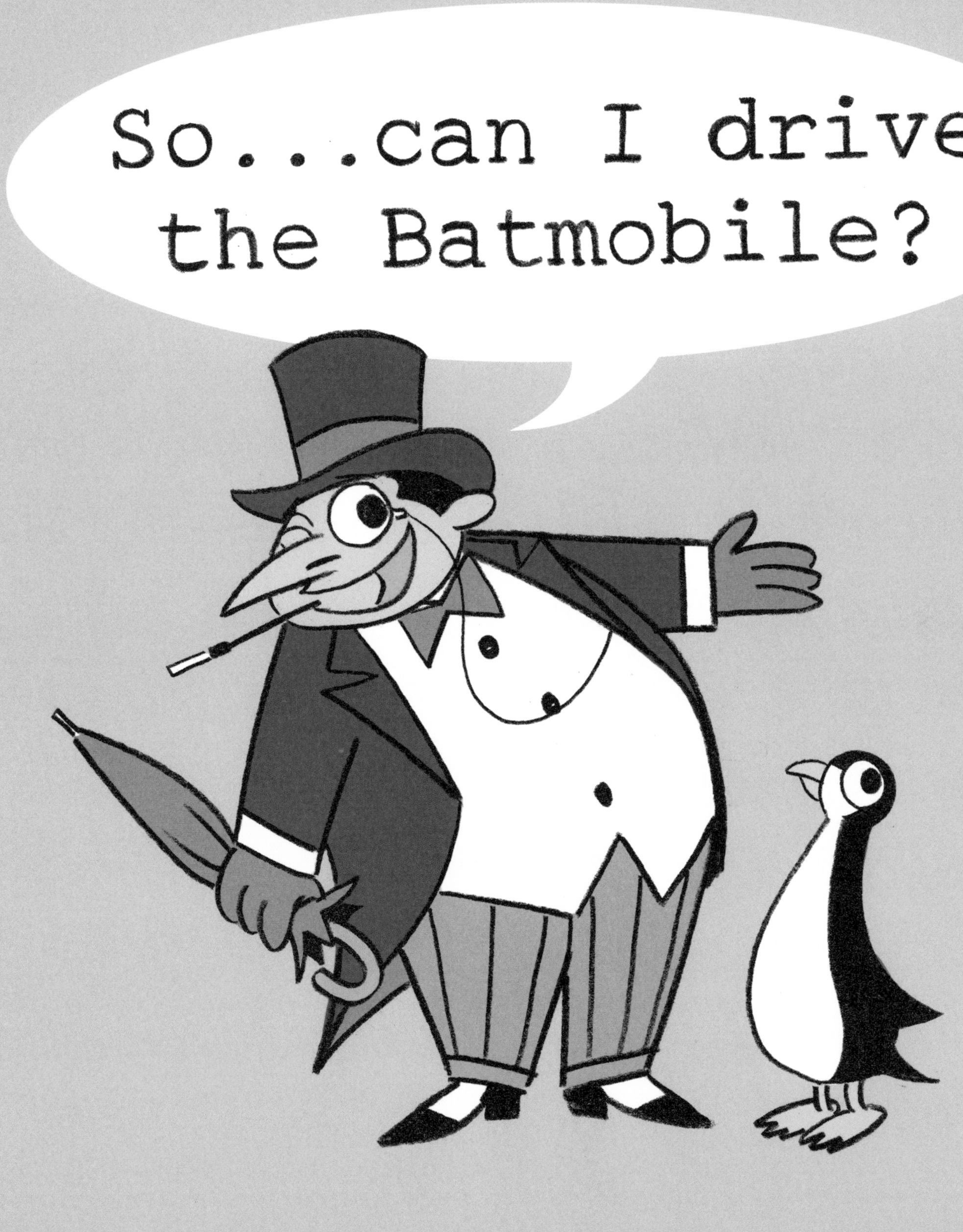
So...can I drive the Batmobile?

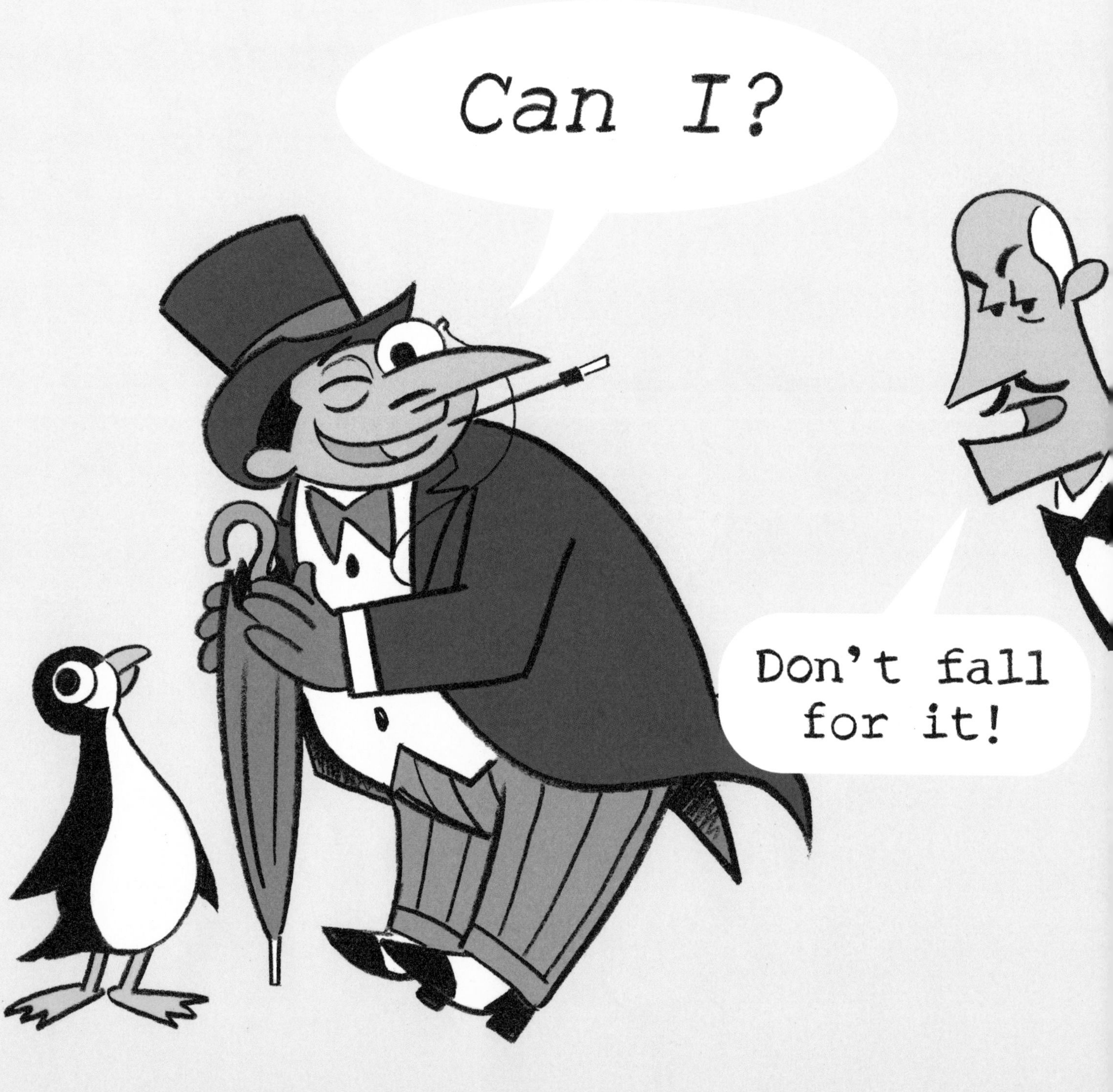
Can I?
Don't fall for it!

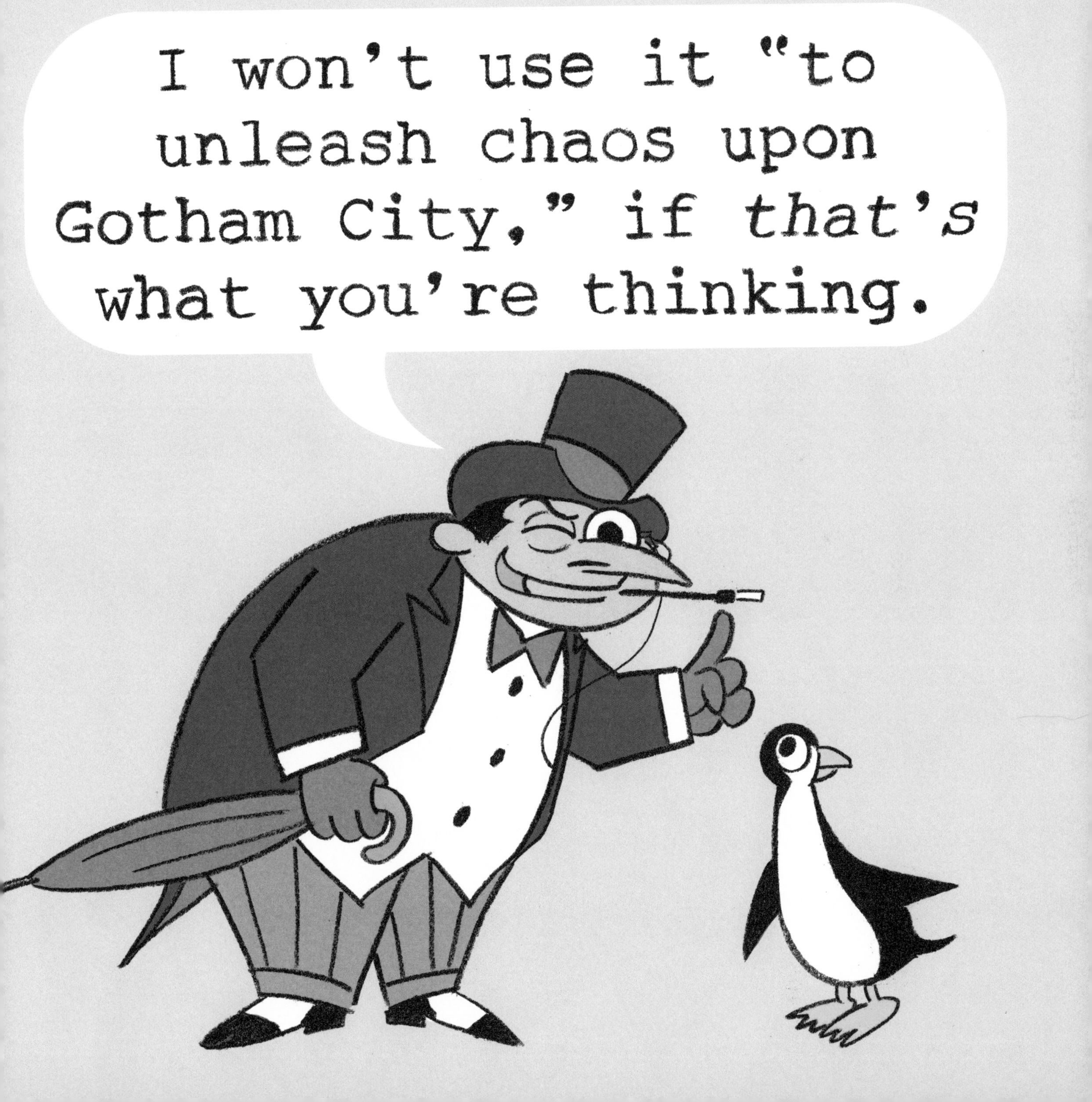
I won't use it "to unleash chaos upon Gotham City," if *that's* what you're thinking.

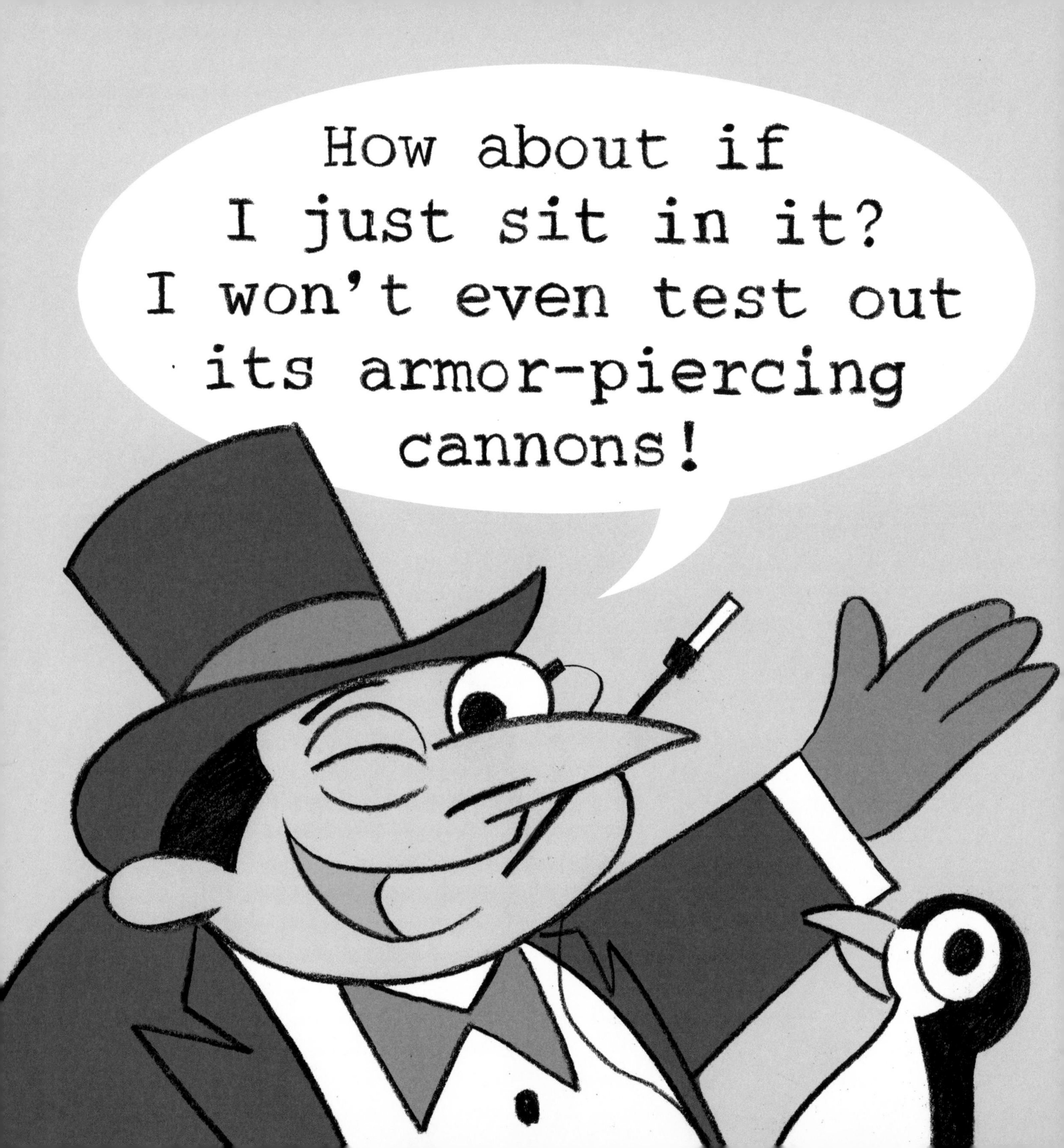
How about if I just sit in it? I won't even test out its armor-piercing cannons!

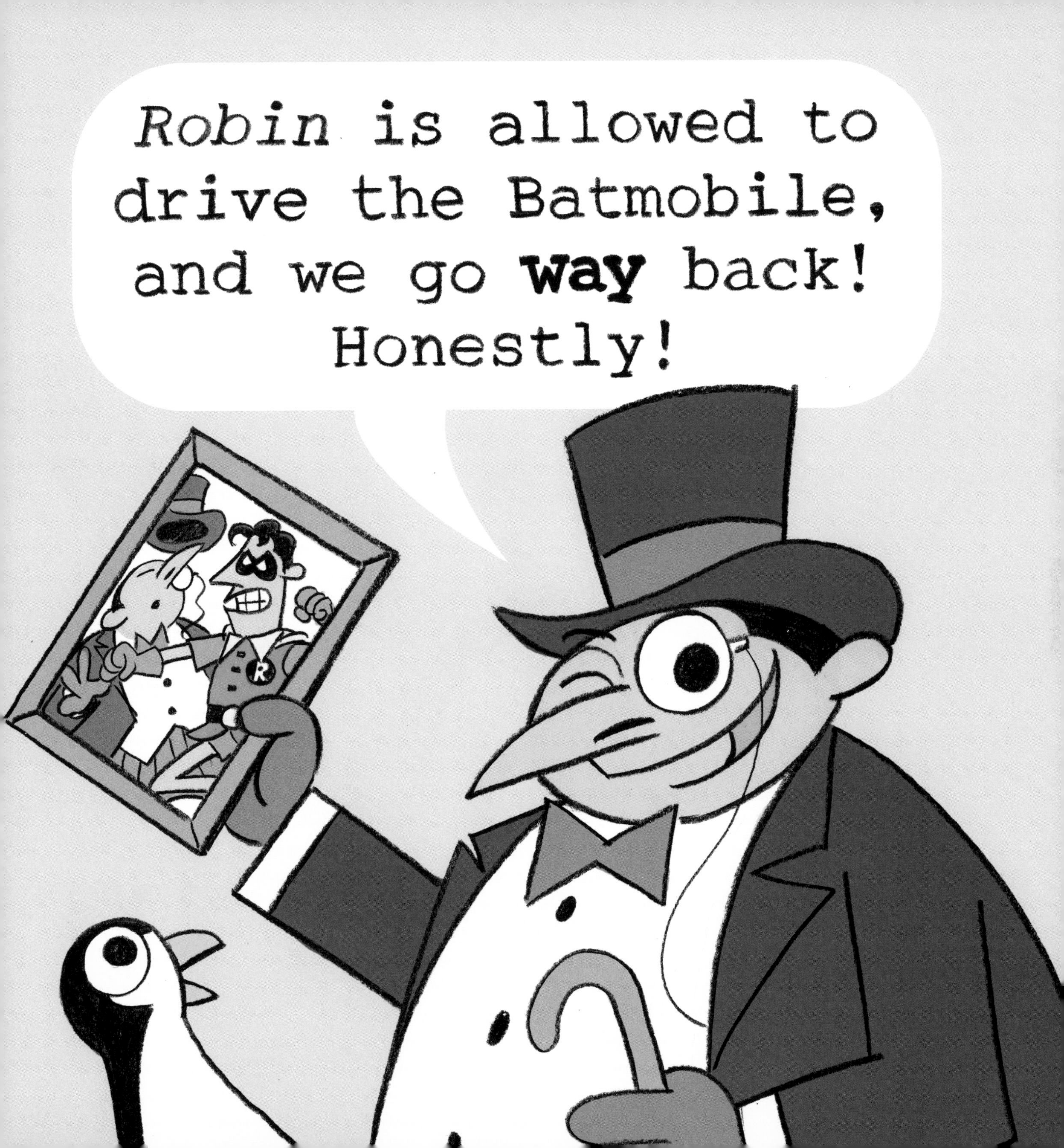
Robin is allowed to drive the Batmobile, and we go **way** back! Honestly!

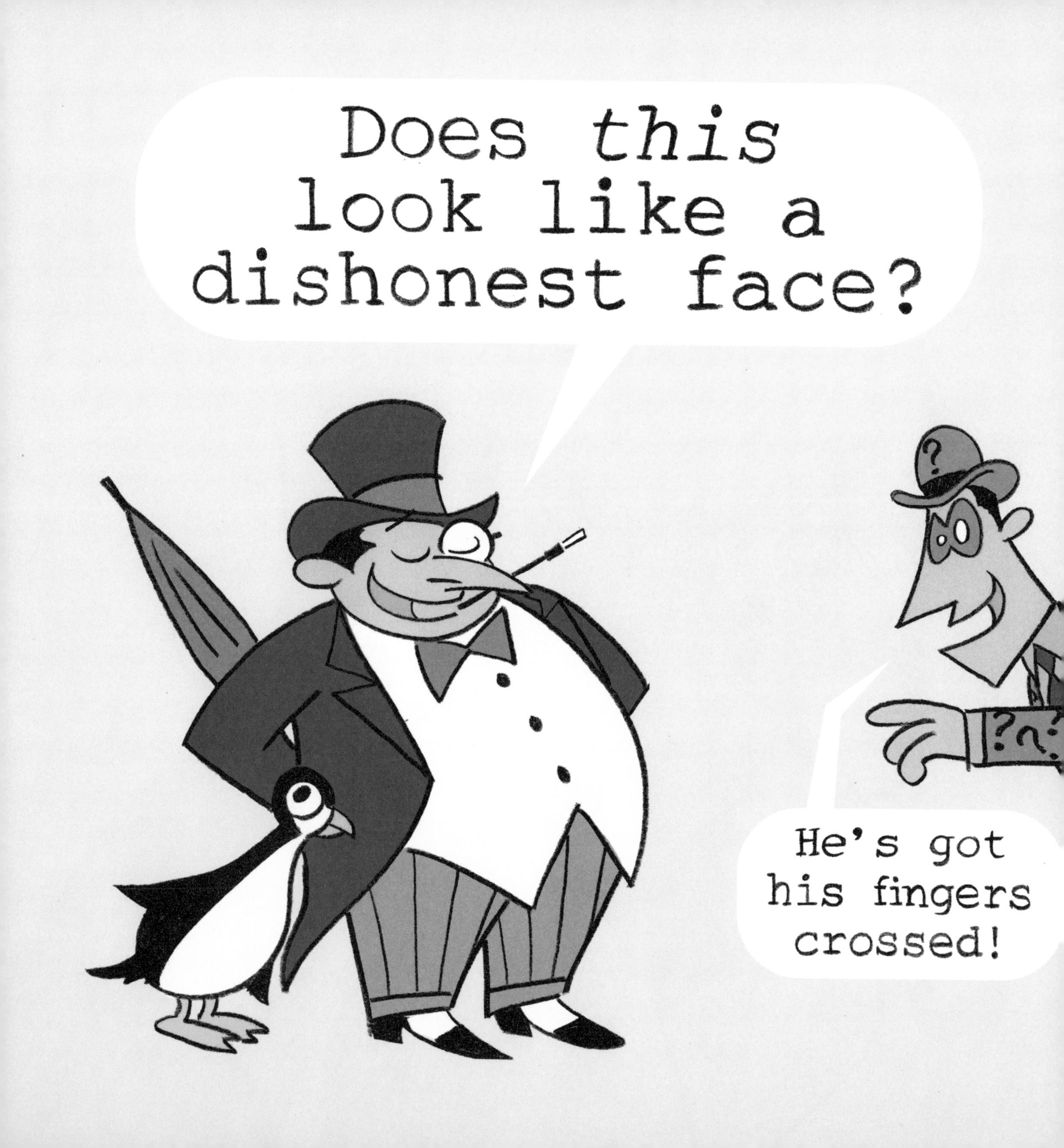
Does *this* look like a dishonest face?
He's got his fingers crossed!

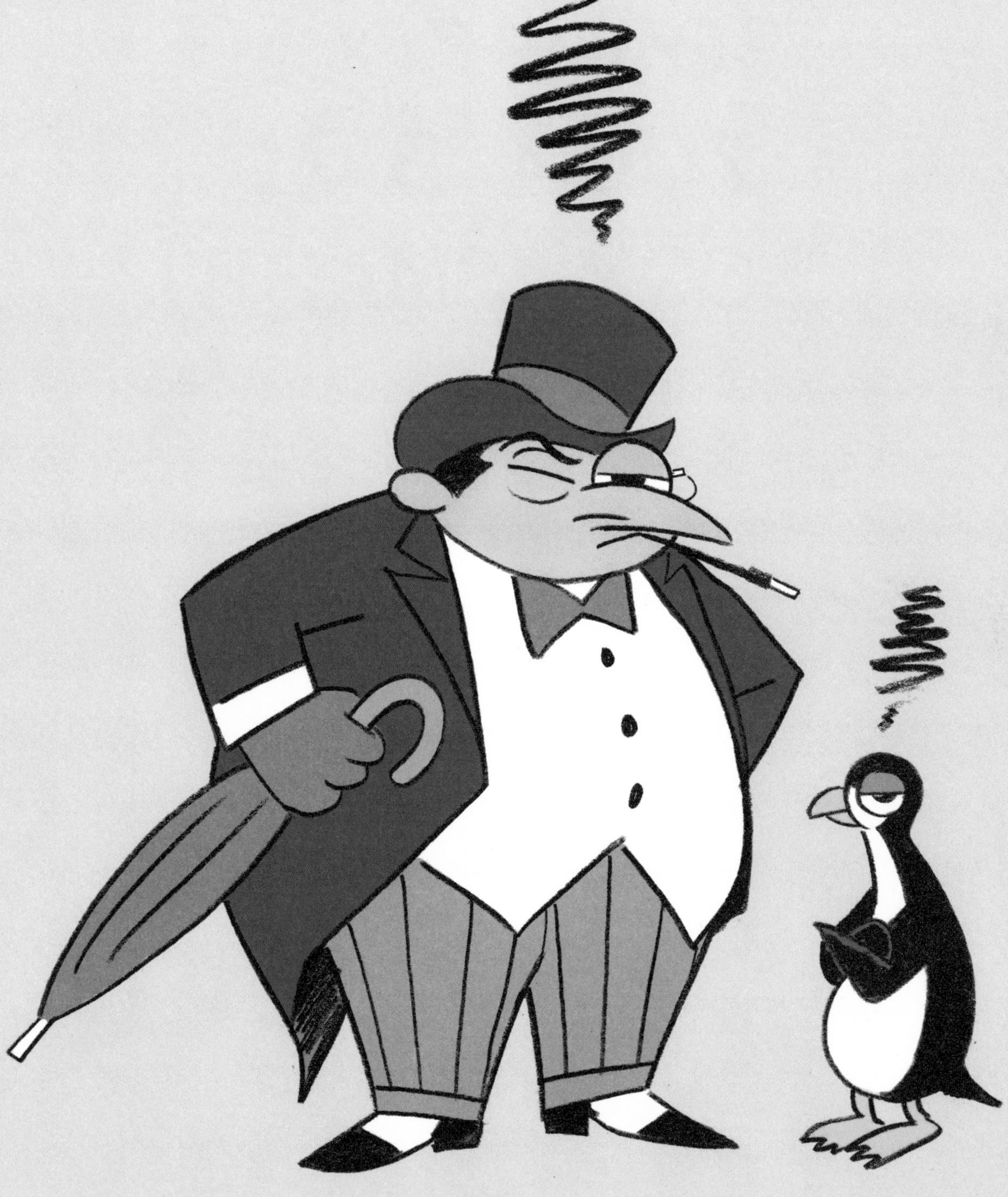

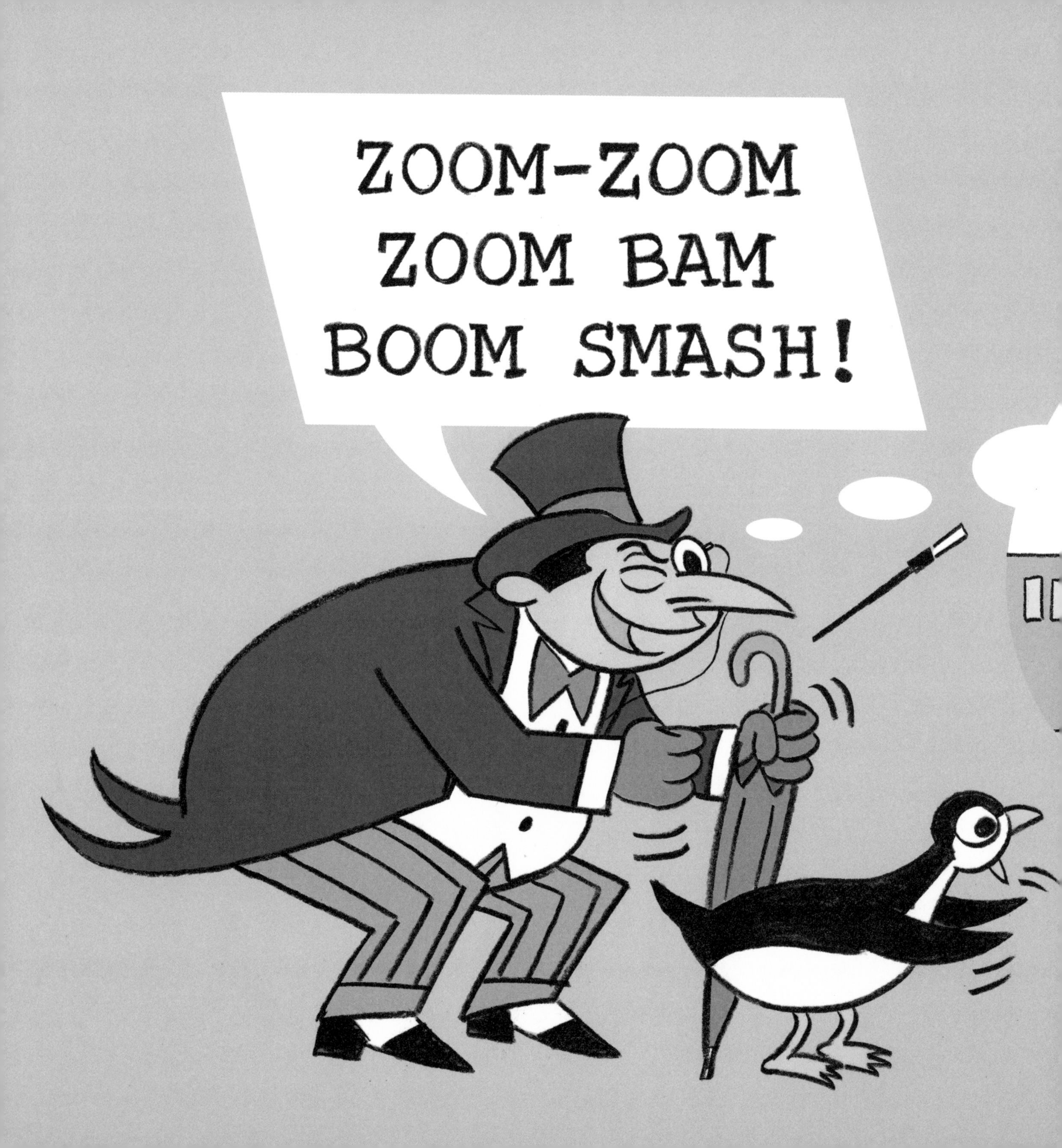
ZOOM-ZOOM ZOOM BAM BOOM SMASH!

PENGUIN
SPEEDING THROUGH
GOTHAM CITY!

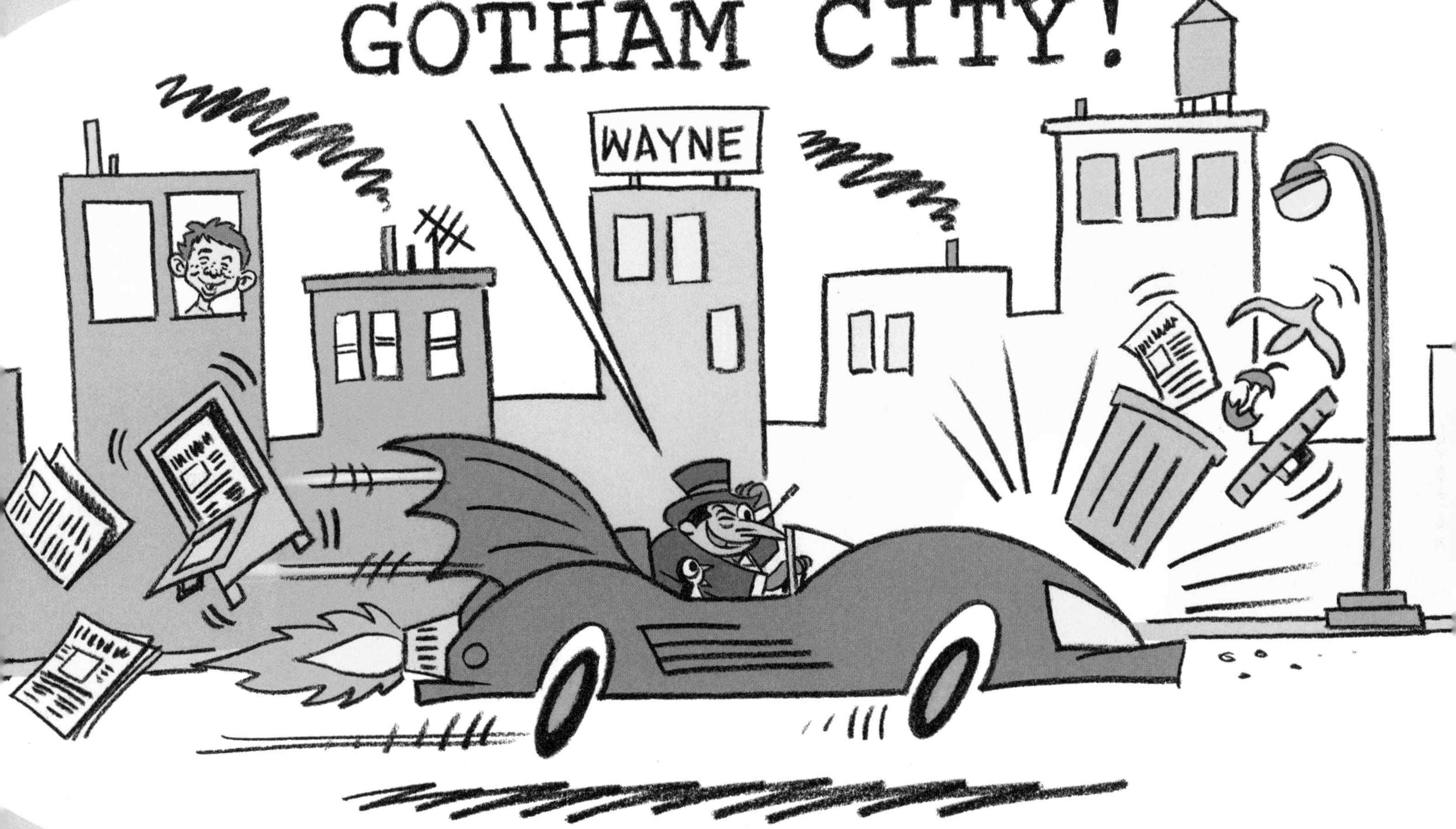
WAYNE

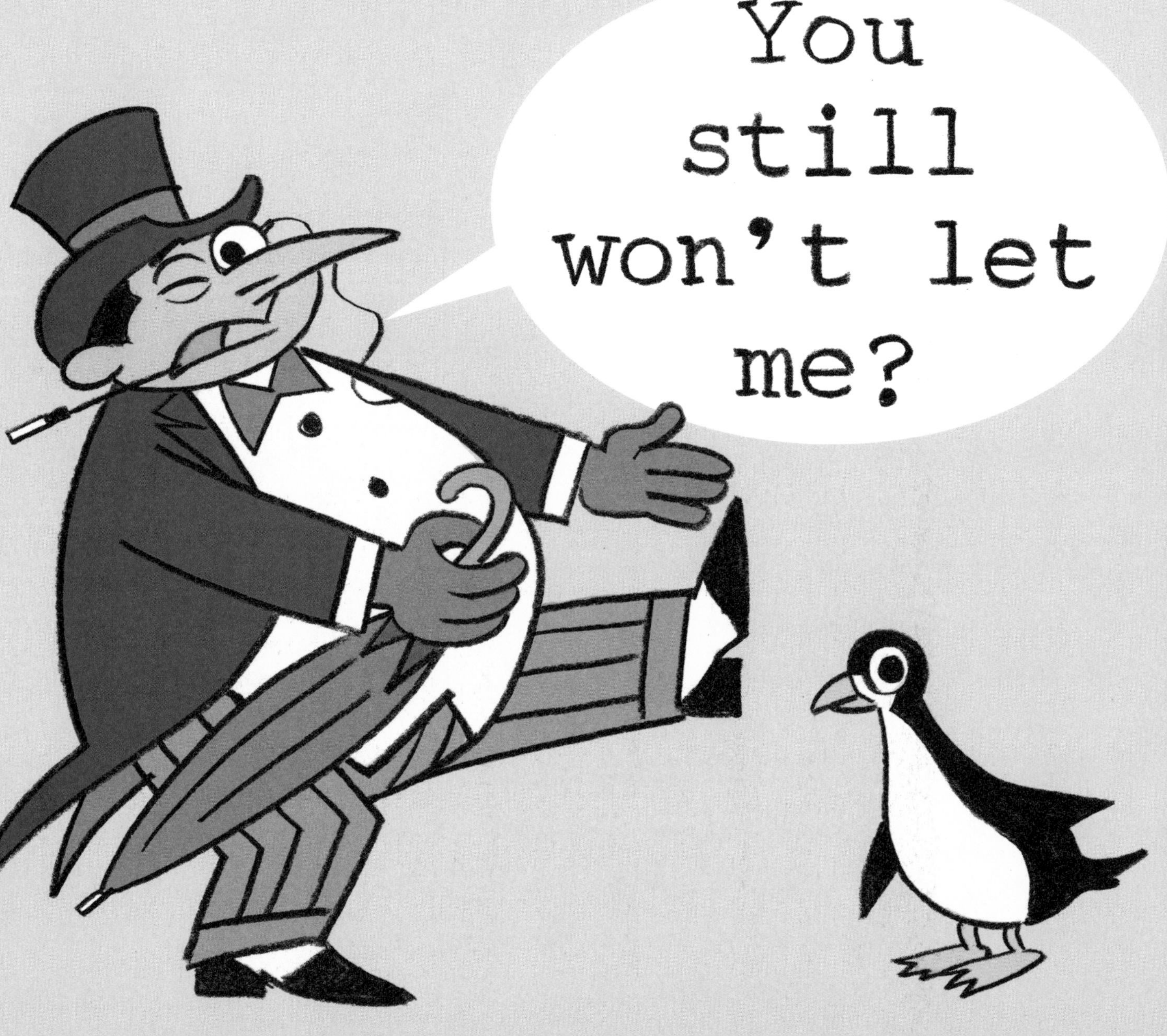
You still won't let me?

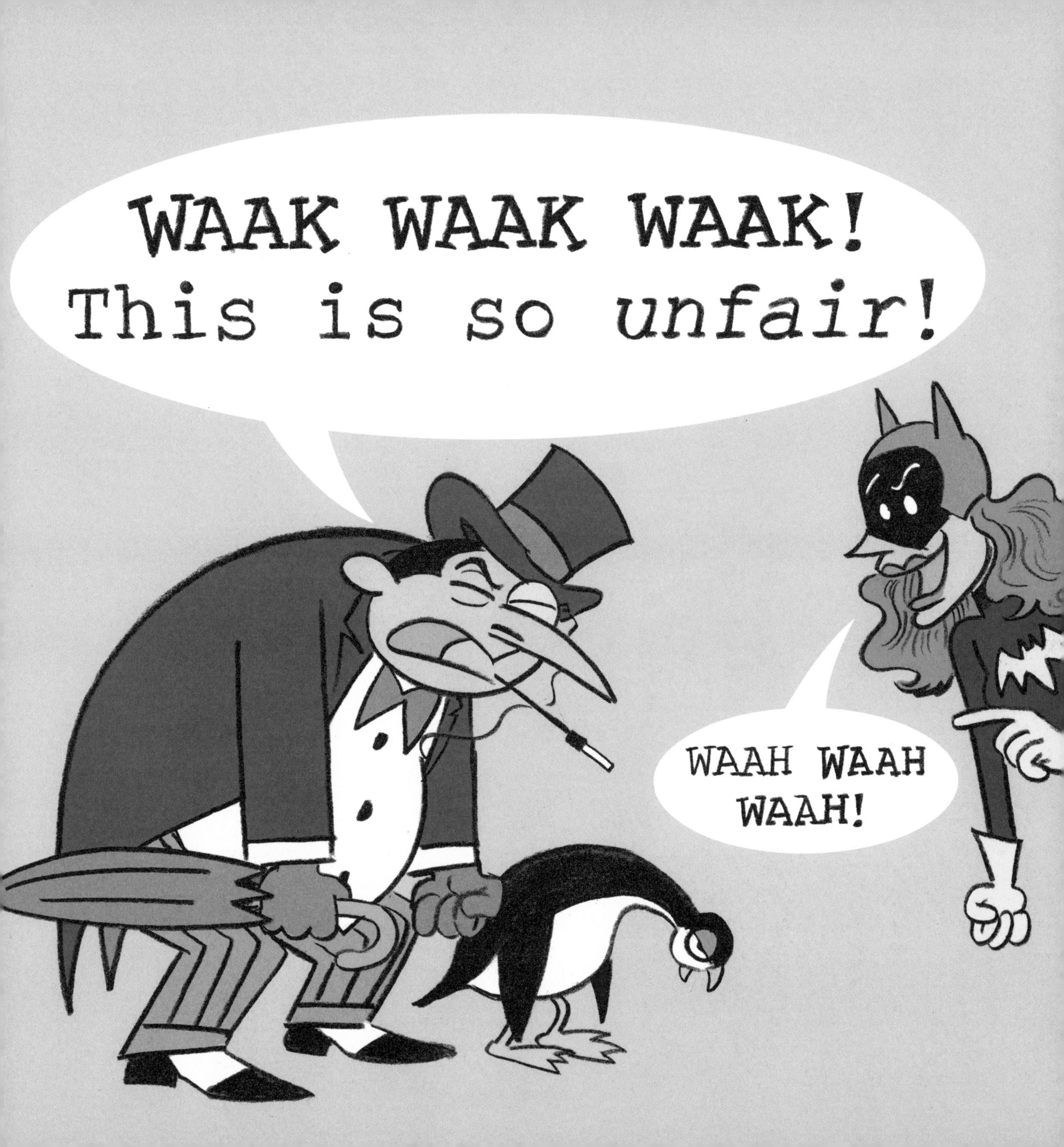
WAAK WAAK WAAK!
This is so *unfair*!
WAAH WAAH
WAAH!

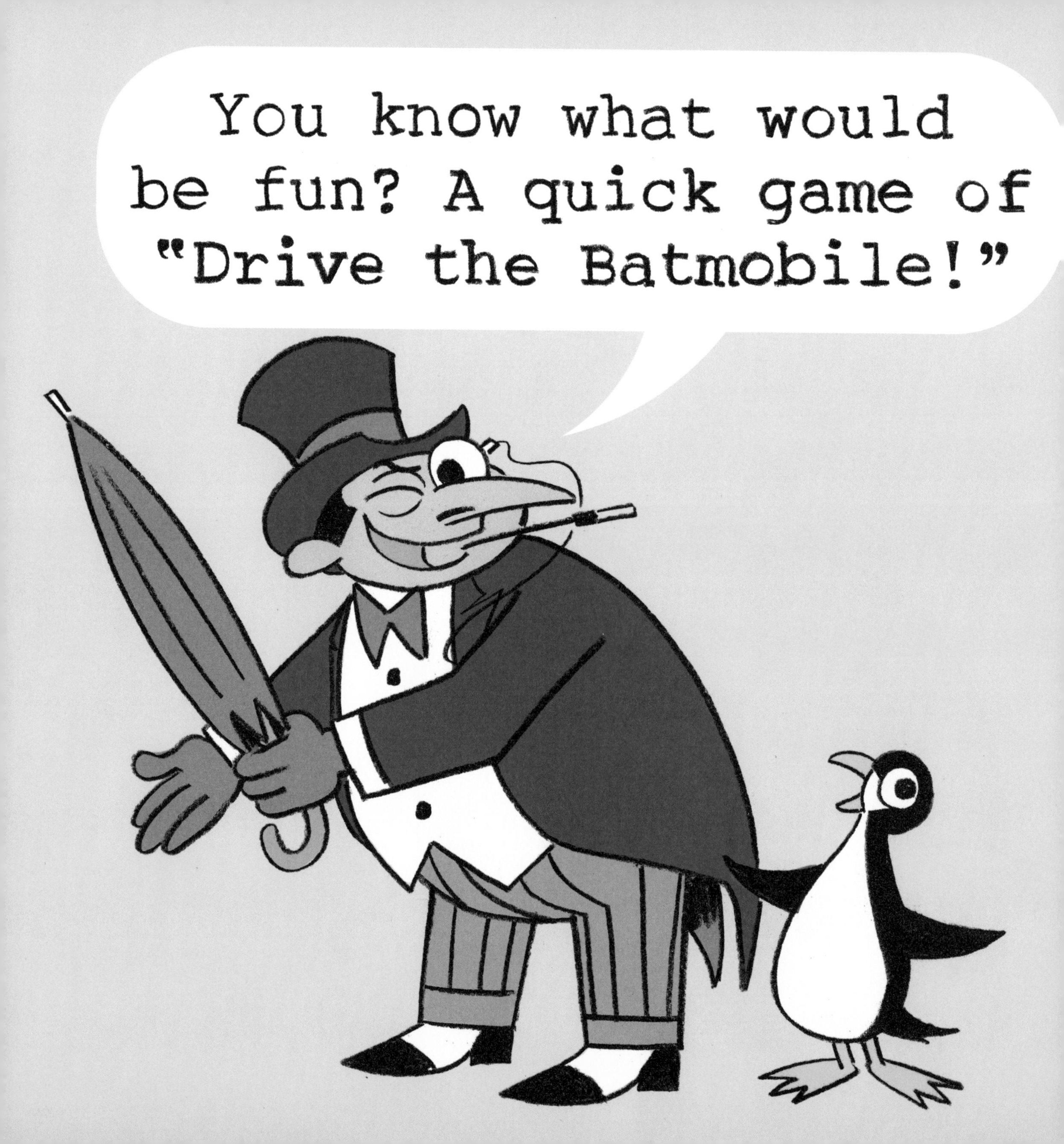
You know what would be fun? A quick game of "Drive the Batmobile!"

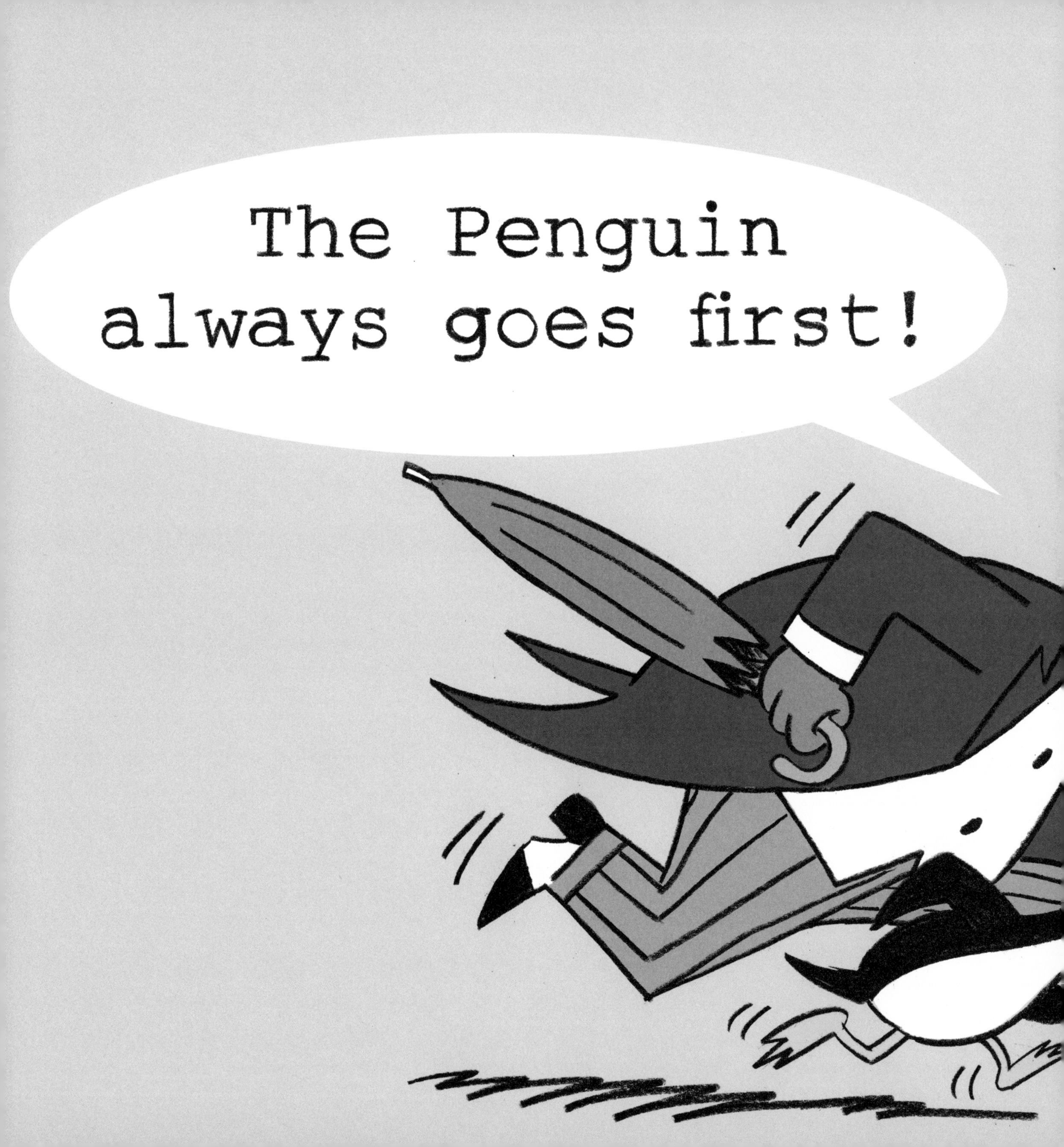
The Penguin always goes first!

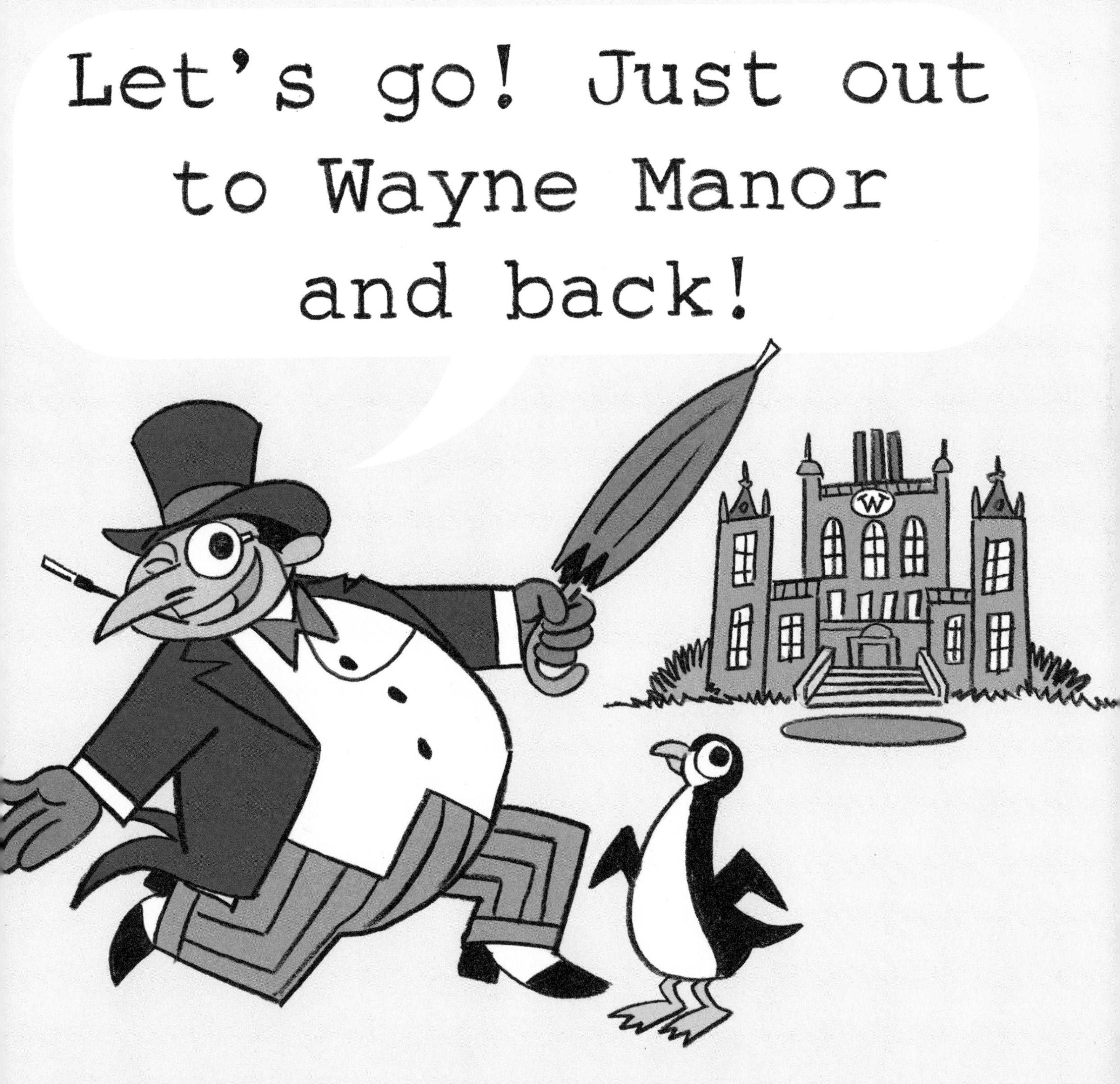
Let's go! Just out to Wayne Manor and back!

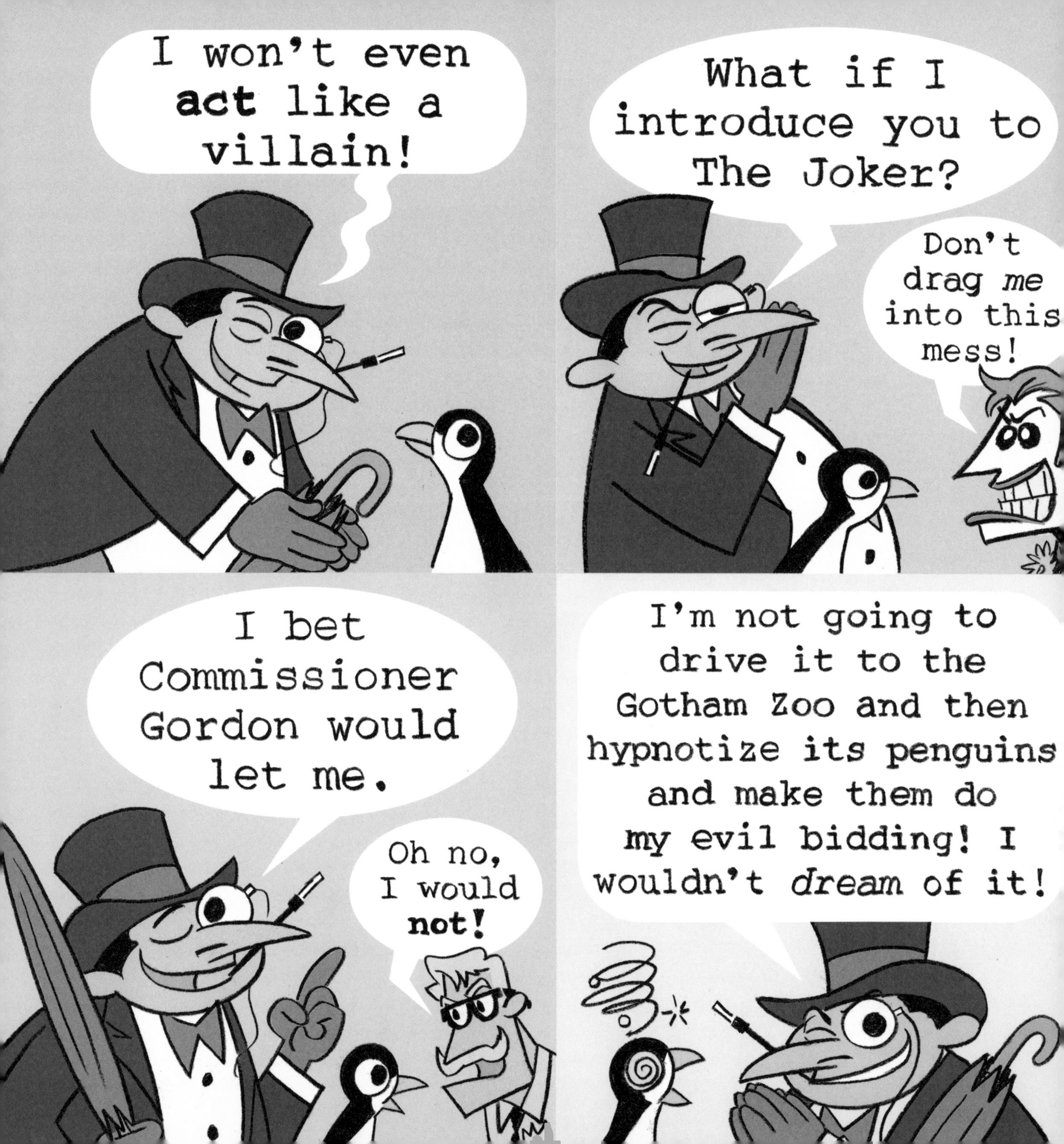
I won't even **act** like a villain!
What if I introduce you to The Joker?
Don't drag *me* into this mess!
I bet Commissioner Gordon would let me.
Oh no, I would **not**!
I'm not going to drive it to the Gotham Zoo and then hypnotize its penguins and make them do my evil bidding! I wouldn't *dream* of it!

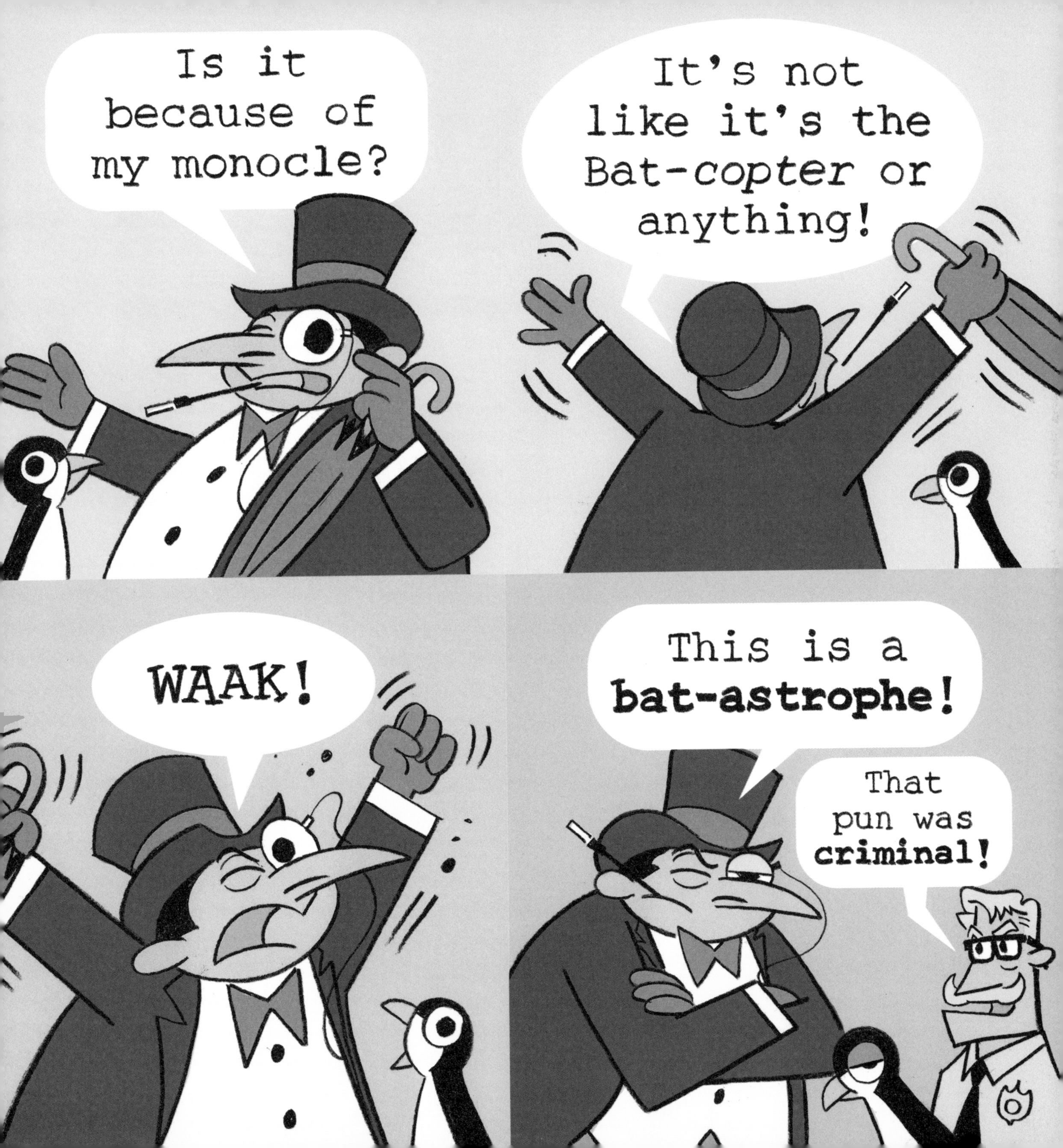
Is it because of my monocle?
It's not like it's the Bat-*copter* or anything!
WAAK!
This is a **bat-astrophe**!
That pun was **criminal**!

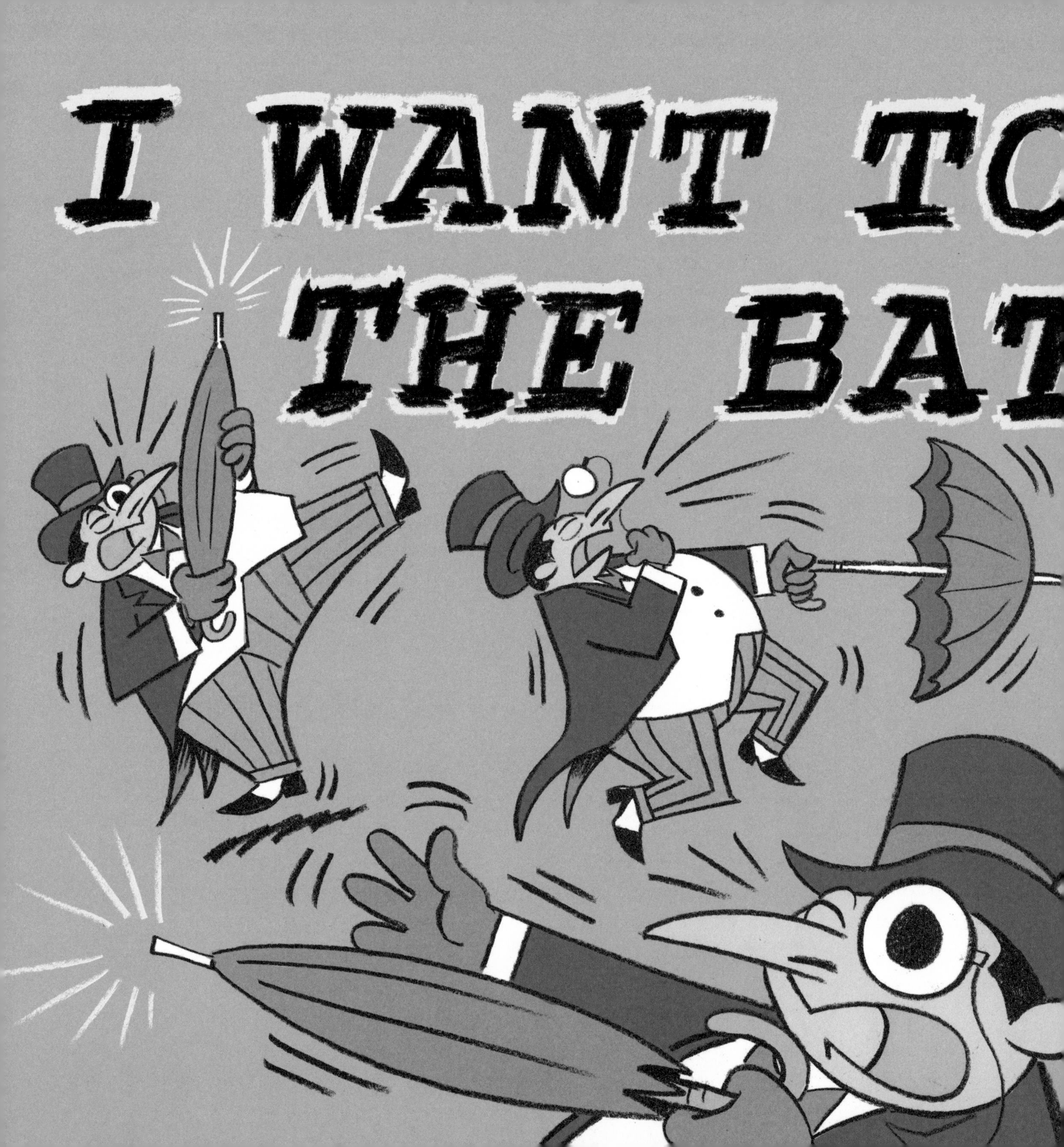
I WANT TO
THE BAT

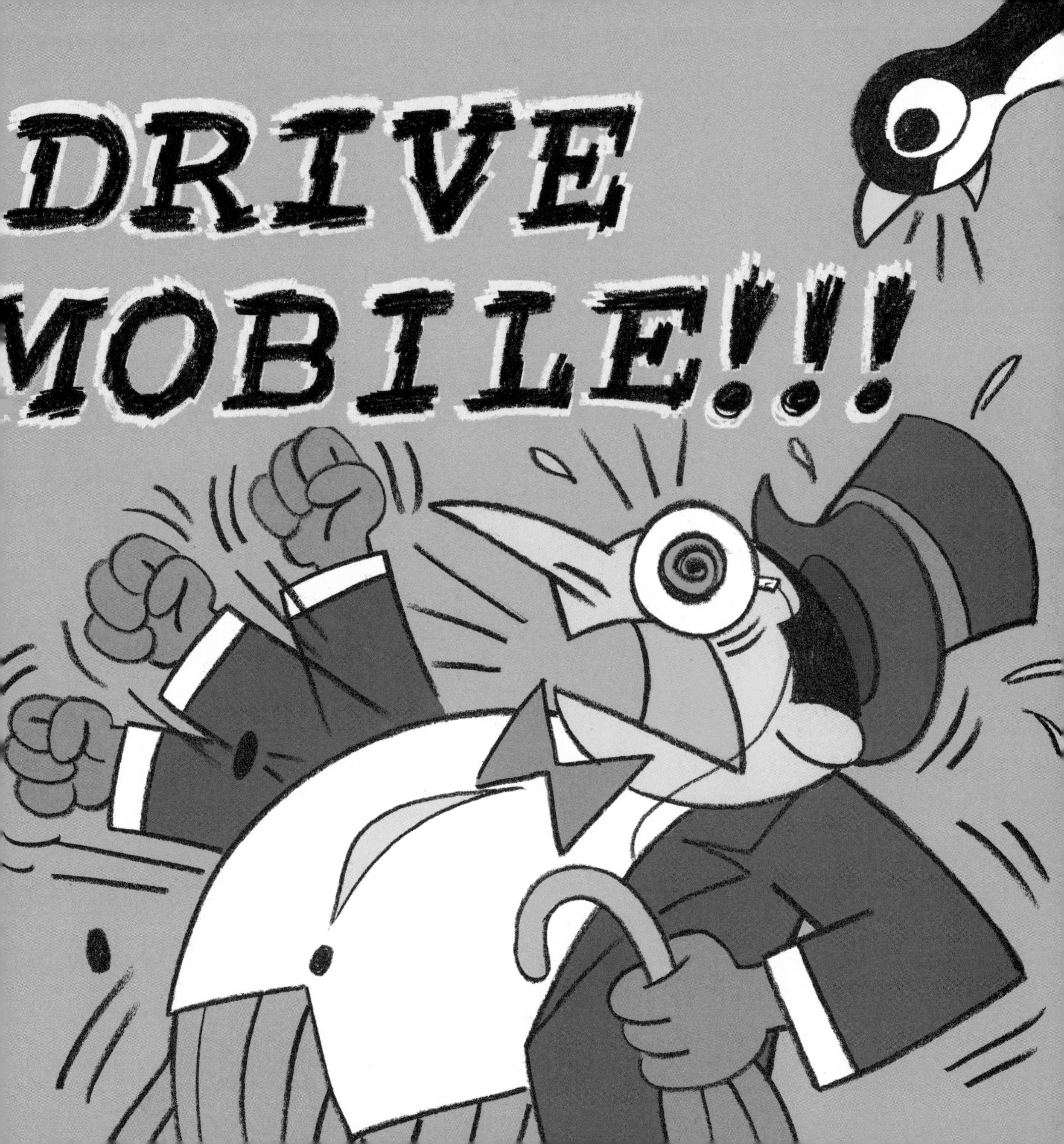
DRIVE
MOBILE!!!

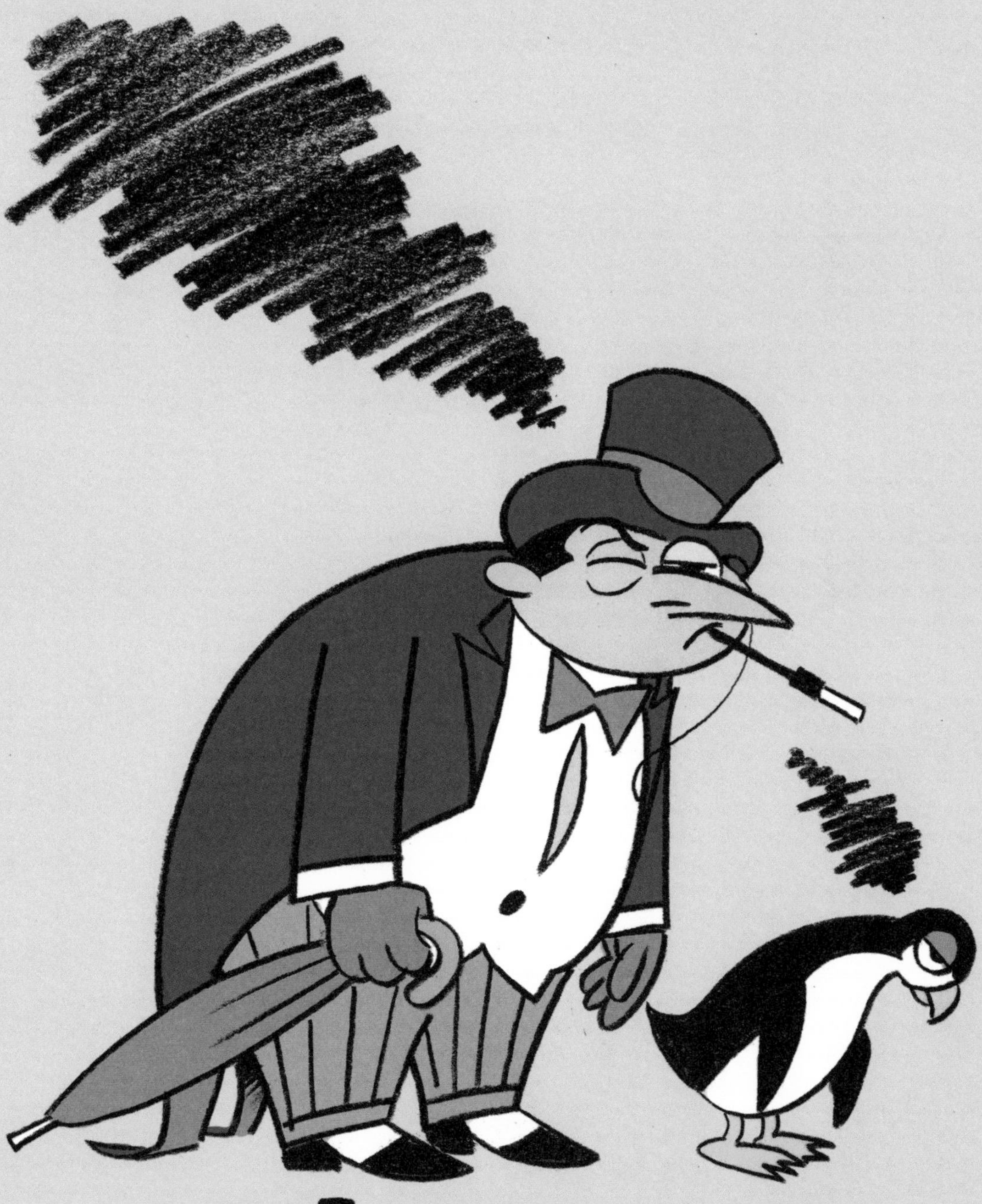

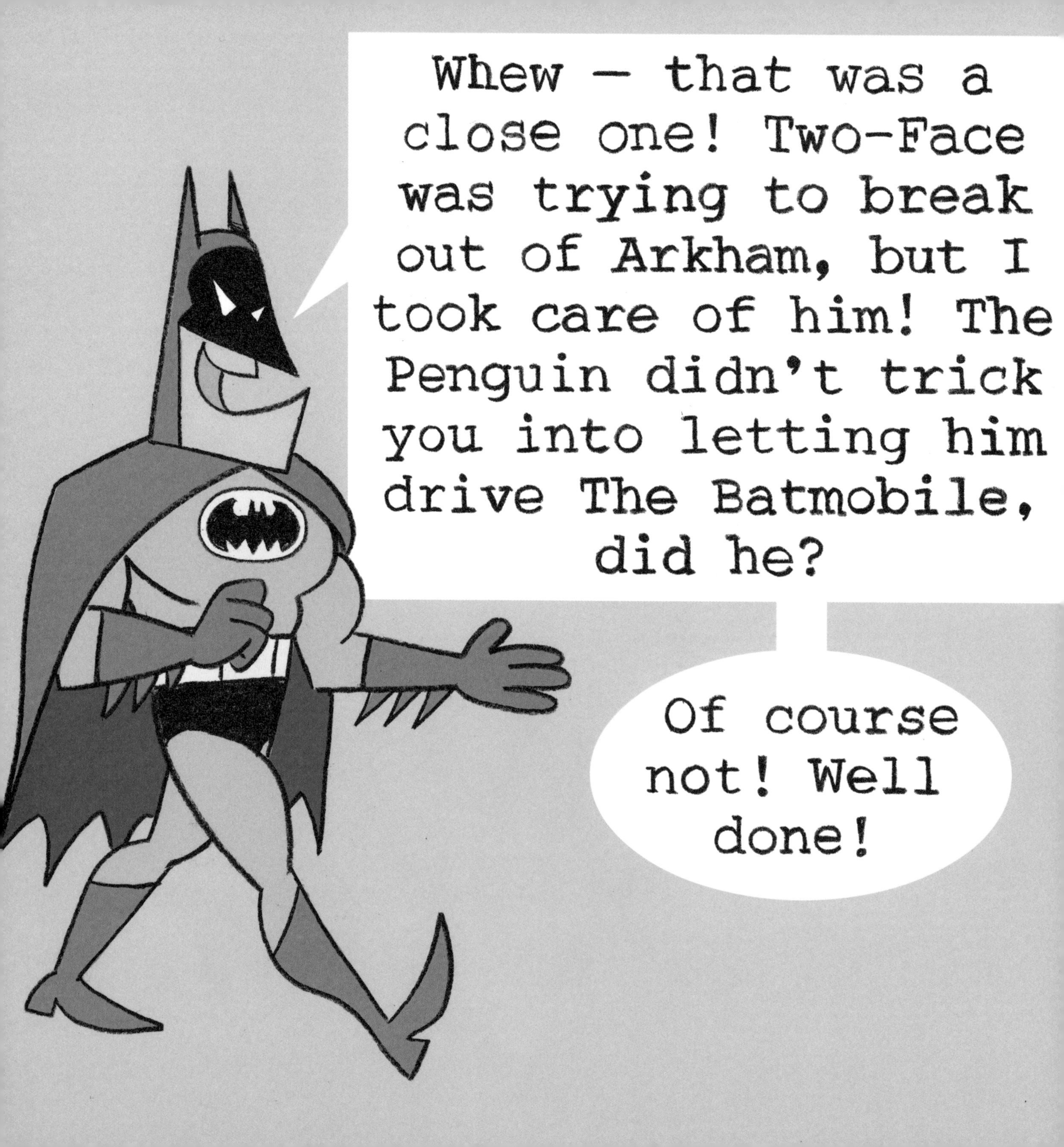
Whew — that was a close one! Two-Face was trying to break out of Arkham, but I took care of him! The Penguin didn't trick you into letting him drive The Batmobile, did he?
Of course not! Well done!

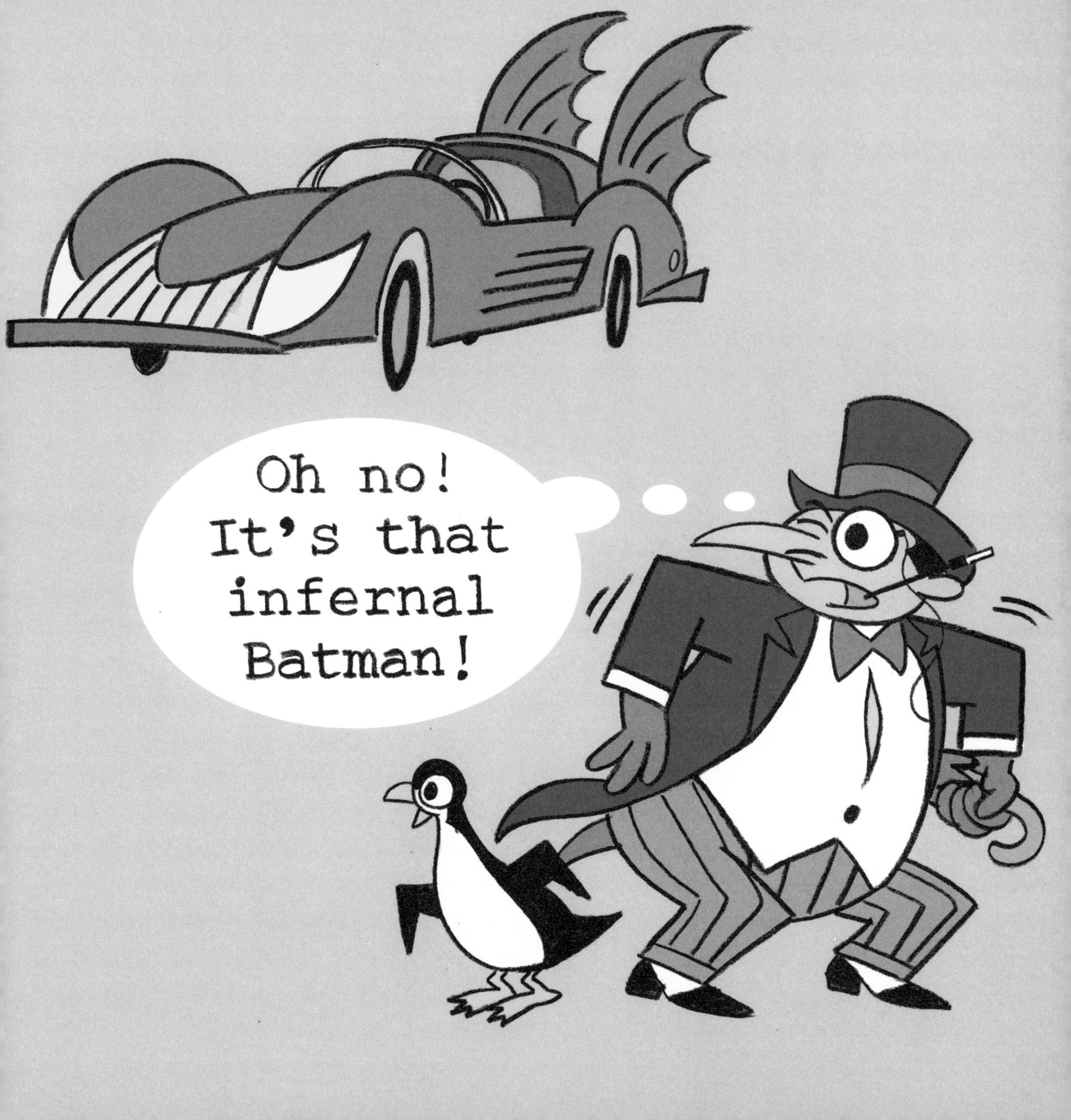
Oh no! It's that infernal Batman!

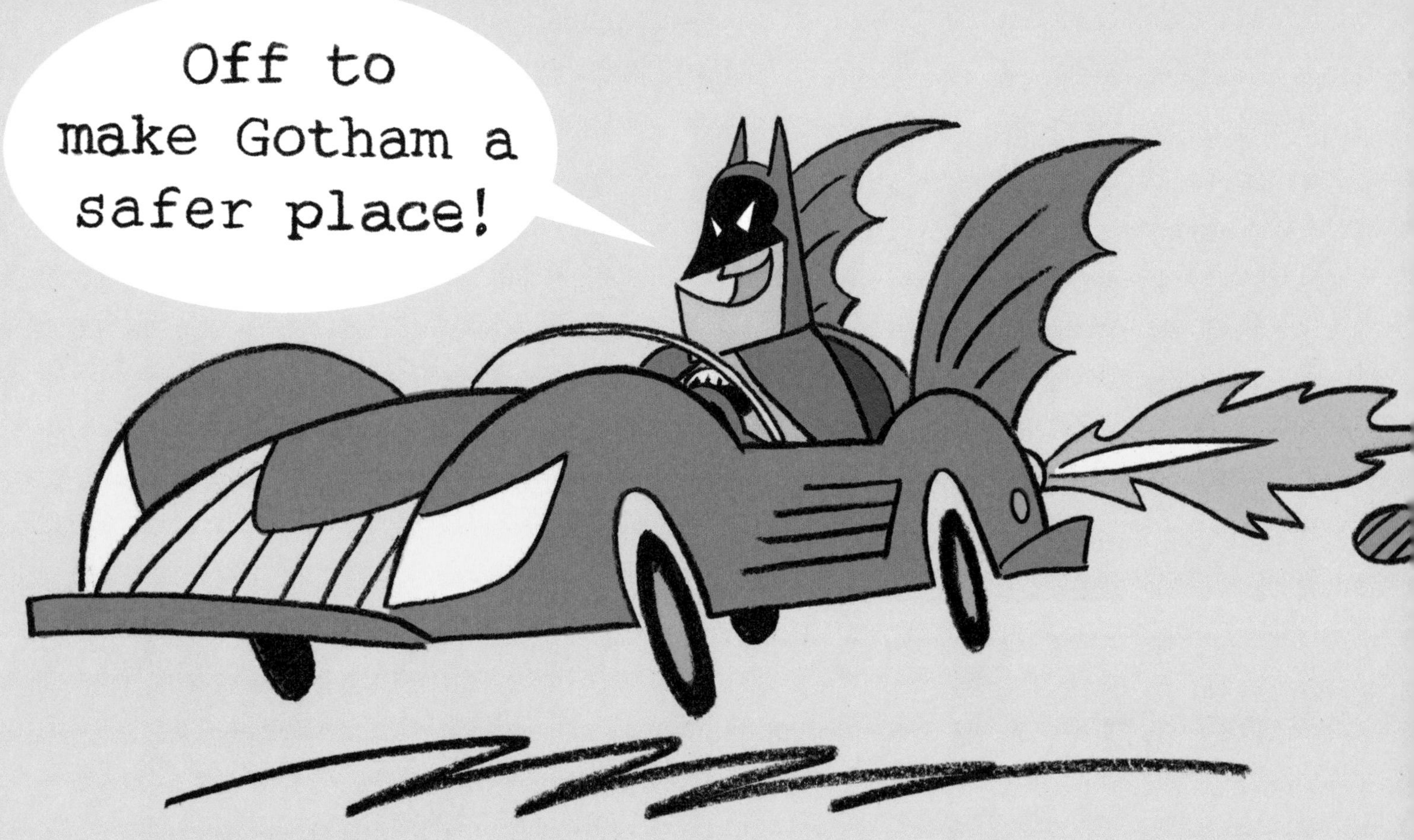
Off to make Gotham a safer place!

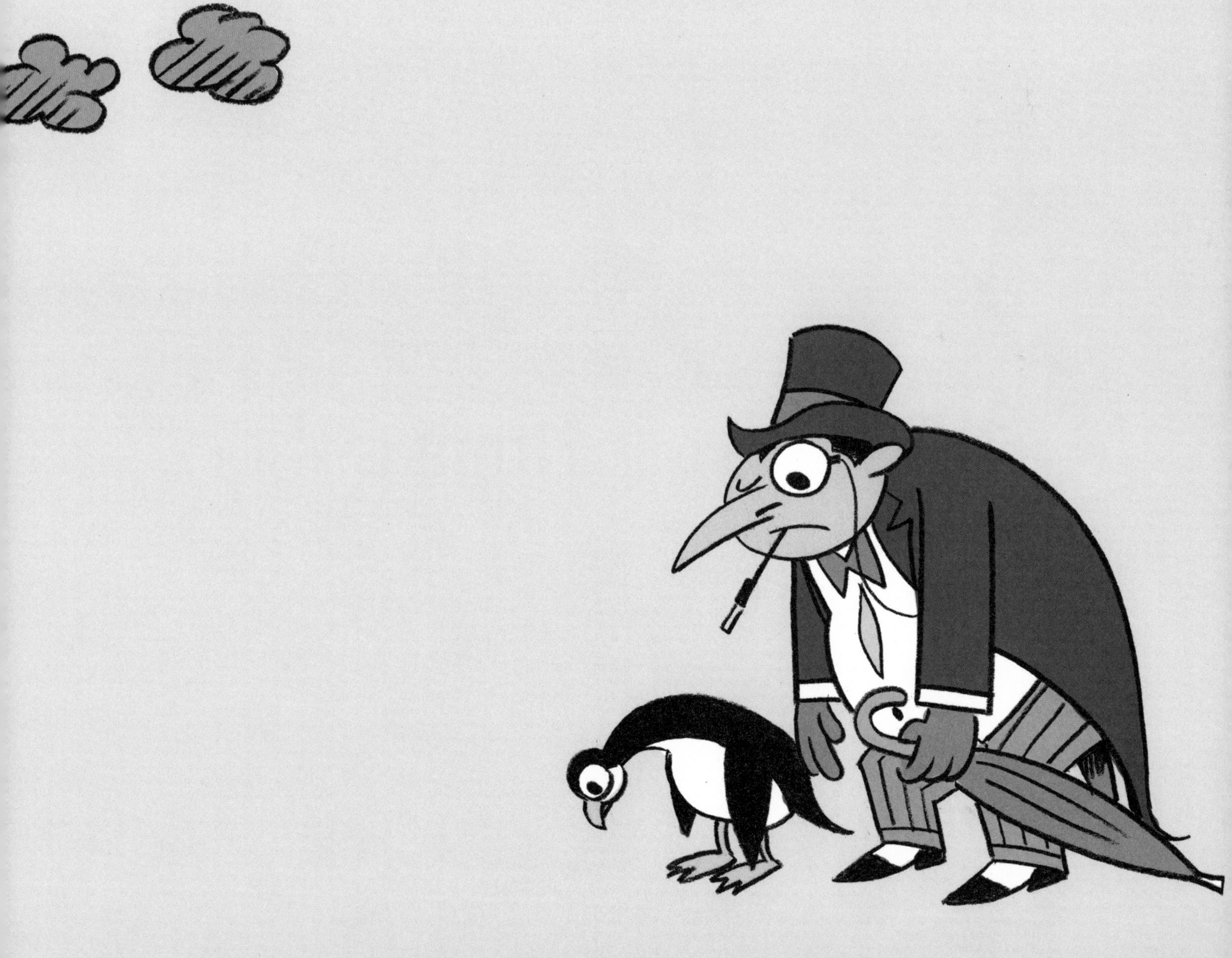

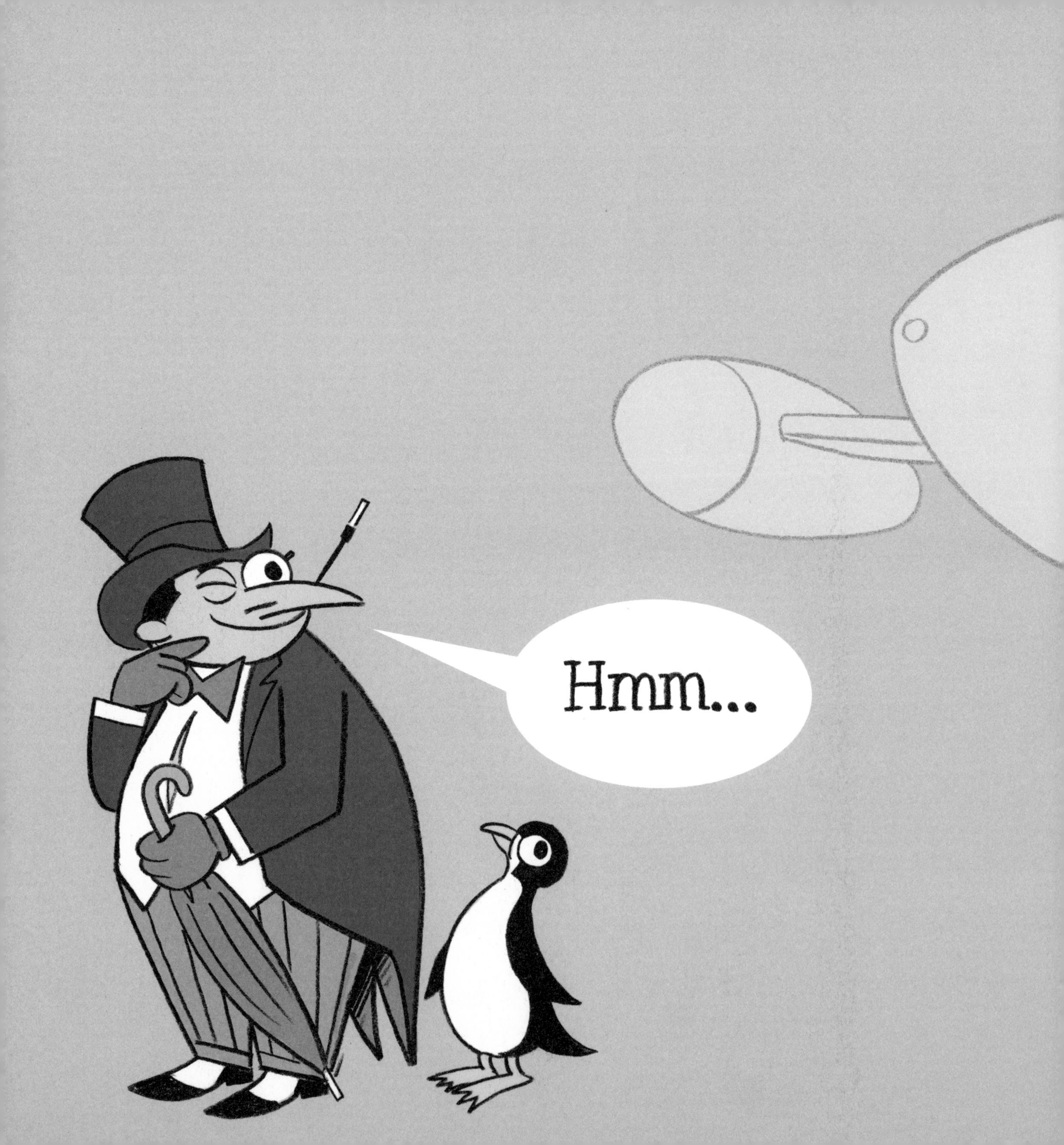
Hmm...